MW01153151

Joseph the Dreamer

HARVEST HOUSE PUBLISHERS
EUGENE, OREGON

The Wonderful Coat

Jacob lived in Canaan. He had eleven sons at the time, but Joseph was his favorite. To show Joseph just how much he loved him, Jacob had a wonderful coat made for him, a long-sleeved robe covered with colorful embroidery.

His brothers were jealous, but what really angered them was when he began telling them of the dreams he had had . . .

Strange Dreams

"Last night I dreamed we were collecting sheaves of grain, when suddenly my sheaf stood up straight and yours all bowed down before it," Joseph told his brothers.

"What are you saying?" they growled. "That you're going to rule over us some day? Go away!"

Joseph had another dream in which the sun and moon and eleven stars were bowing down before him. Even his father was cross when he heard about the latest dream.

"Do you really think that your mother and I and your brothers are going to bow down to you? Don't get too big for your boots!"

But Jacob did secretly wonder to himself about what Joseph's dream might mean.

Thrown into a Well

Joseph's brothers had had enough! What with the fabulous coat and now these dreadful dreams, they felt the time had come to get rid of their annoying brother.

One day, when they were out in the fields, the brothers set upon him, tearing off his precious multicolored coat and throwing him in a deep pit. Then they sat down nearby to eat, deaf to his cries for help!

Sold into Slavery

Soon they saw a caravan of Ishmaelite traders passing by on their camels on their way to Egypt, and quick as a flash they decided to sell him to the traders.

Then they took his beautiful coat and ripped it into pieces, and they killed a goat and smeared the coat with blood. Once this was done, they trooped home with long faces and showed the ruined coat to their father, saying that Joseph had been killed by a wild animal!

Poor Joseph was heartbroken at the death of his beloved son.

Potiphar's Wife

Joseph had been sold to one of Pharaoh's officials, a man named Potiphar, but God was still looking after him. Joseph was clever and hardworking, and soon Potiphar placed him in charge of his whole household.

But the peaceful times didn't last, for Potiphar's wife took a liking to Joseph. Joseph tried to have nothing to do with her, but one day when he pulled away from her, in his haste he left his coat behind. When her husband came back, she showed him the coat and told him that Joseph had come to her bedroom to take advantage of her, and had run away when she screamed.

Potiphar was furious and threw poor Joseph into jail!

The Steward's Dream

Some time later, both Pharaoh's wine steward and his chief baker angered Pharaoh and were thrown into prison along with Joseph.

One night, both men had strange dreams and were puzzled. Joseph told them, "My God will be able to help. Tell me your dreams."

The wine steward went first. "In my dream I saw a vine with three branches covered in grapes. I took the grapes and squeezed them into Pharaoh's cup."

Joseph told him that within three days Pharaoh would forgive him and take him back. "Please remember me when he does!" he said to the wine steward.

The Baker Gets a Nasty Shock

Now the baker was anxious to tell his dream too. "On my head were three baskets of bread," he said, "but birds were eating Pharaoh's pastries."

Joseph was sad. He really didn't want to have to tell the baker what his dream meant. "Within three days Pharaoh will cut off your head, and the birds will eat your flesh," he said reluctantly.

Things turned out just as Joseph had foretold, for in three days it was Pharaoh's birthday, and on that day he pardoned the wine steward and gave him back his job, but he executed the chief baker!

The wine steward forgot all about Joseph though.

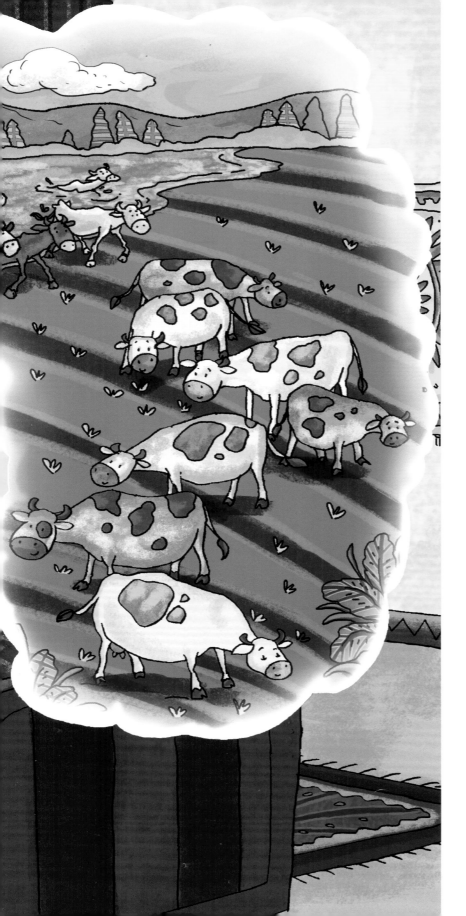

Pharaoh's Strange Dream

Two years passed by. Then one night, Pharaoh, the king of Egypt, had a strange dream. He was standing by the Nile when out of the river came seven fat, healthy-looking cows, and they grazed among the reeds. Then seven other cows came up out of the Nile. These cows were ugly and thin. They ate up the fat cows and yet looked just as thin and sickly as before!

Pharaoh had another dream. In this dream, seven healthy heads of grain were growing on a single stalk. Then seven more heads of grain sprouted, and these were thin and scorched by the wind. But the thin heads of grain swallowed up the seven healthy, full heads!

Can You Help?

In the morning, Pharaoh felt worried. He sent for all the magicians and wise men of Egypt, but no one could tell him what his strange dreams might mean.

It was only then that the wine steward remembered Joseph. The slave was brought before mighty Pharaoh, who asked him to explain his dreams.

"I cannot do it," Joseph humbly replied to Pharaoh, "but God will be able to explain."

And so Pharaoh told Joseph all about his dreams.

The Meaning of the Dream

Joseph told Pharaoh, "The two dreams are really one and the same. The seven cows and the seven heads of grain are seven years. The land will be blessed with seven years of healthy crops and fine harvests, but they will be followed by seven years of dreadful famine. You will need to plan very carefully to prepare."

Pharaoh spoke to his advisors and then turned to Joseph, saying, "Clearly you are the man for the job! I will put you in charge of my land, and you will be second only to me in all of Egypt!"

And with that, Pharaoh put his own signet ring on Joseph's finger, placed a gold chain around his neck, and dressed him in fine clothes!

Planning for the Famine

Joseph traveled throughout the land, riding in a fine chariot, to make sure that food was put aside for the hard times ahead. Just as he had foretold, for seven years the crops grew better than ever before, and so much grain was put away in big storehouses that he gave up counting it!

After seven years, the famine began. When people began to run out of food, Joseph opened up the storehouses and sold the corn. No one in Egypt went hungry. In fact, there was so much food that people from other countries came to buy it, for the famine was bad everywhere.

The Brothers Come to Egypt

Joseph's brothers were among those who came to buy grain, for the famine had been bad in Canaan too. Only his youngest brother, Benjamin, had stayed behind. The brothers bowed down before Joseph. With his golden chain and fine clothes, they did not recognize him at all!

Joseph wanted to see if his brothers had changed, and so he decided to test them. He agreed to let all of them except Simeon go back home with corn, but only if they returned with their youngest brother.

Jacob did not want to let Benjamin go, but in the end he had to agree, and so all ten brothers returned to Egypt.

Treachery

The test wasn't over. Joseph had his servants feed the brothers, and then he sent them on their way with more corn, but not before hiding a silver cup in Benjamin's sack.

The brothers were traveling home when guards came and dragged them back to the palace.

"Thieves!" shouted Joseph. "You repay my kindness by stealing!"

"There must be some mistake!" cried the brothers, but when the guards checked, there was the silver cup in Benjamin's sack!

The brothers fell to their knees. "My lord," they cried, "take any one of us, but do not take Benjamin, for his father's heart would break!"

Forgiven

At this, Joseph knew that his brothers really had changed. They cared so much for their little brother and for how upset their father would be, that any one of them would have given himself up to save Benjamin.

Crying tears of joy, Joseph went to hug them and told them who he really was! He told them not to feel too bad about what had happened, for it had all been part of God's plan. "I was sent to rule in Egypt so that you would not starve in Canaan!" he said.

At first, they could hardly believe that this great man was their long-lost brother, but when they did, they were filled with joy, for they had had many years to feel sorry for what they had done.

Reunited

Now it was time to tell Jacob the good news. When the brothers returned saying that his beloved son Joseph was not only alive and well, but governor of all Egypt, old Jacob could hardly believe his ears! But when he saw all the fine gifts that Joseph had sent him, he had to believe his eyes!

Then Jacob gathered up all his belongings, his herds and flocks, and he and all his family traveled to Egypt where Pharaoh had promised them good farmland.

Joseph came to meet his father in a great chariot, and the reunion was just as happy and as emotional as you could possibly imagine!

Joseph the Dreamer

©2014 (North America) International Publishing
Services Pty Ltd. Sydney Australia.
www.ipsoz.com , External Markets © NPP Ltd Bath

Published by Harvest House Publishers
Eugene, Oregon 97402
www.harvesthousepublishers.com

ISBN 978-0-7369-6156-1

All rights reserved. No part of this publication may be reproduced, stored in a retrieval system, or
transmitted in any form or by any means—electronic, mechanical, digital, photocopy, recording, or any
other—except for brief quotations in printed reviews, without the prior permission of the publisher.

Printed in China

14 15 16 17 18 19 20 21 / IPS / 10 9 8 7 6 5 4 3 2 1